30 Days of Rest for Mothers

a devotional

Susan Brown

This is a work of nonfiction.

Copyright ©2022 Susan Brown

ISBN: 978-0-6456057-0-9

All rights reserved. No part of this book may be reproduced, stored in a retrieval system, or transmitted in any form or by any means–electronic, mechanical, photocopy, recording, or any other–except for brief quotations for book reviews, without written permission of the author.

First paperback edition November 2022

Unless otherwise noted, Bible quotations are taken from HOLY BIBLE, NEW INTERNATIONAL VERSION®, NIV® Copyright© 1973, 1978, 1984, 2011 by Biblica, Inc.™ Used by permission. All rights reserved worldwide.

Quotations marked International Standard Version are taken from The Holy Bible: International Standard Version® U.S. English Imprint Release 2.0 Copyright © 1996-2013 The ISV Foundation. Used by permission. All rights reserved internationally.

Quotations marked New King James Version are taken from The Holy Bible: New King James Version®. Copyright © 1982 by Thomas Nelson. Used by permission. All rights reserved.

Book cover design by Claire van Ryn, Inkling Media

Book design by aalishaa (Fiverr)

Dedication

*To all mothers who
long to abide in the rest of God.*

'Whoever dwells in the shelter of the Most High will rest in the shadow of the Almighty.'

Psalm 91:1

Table of Contents

Welcome vii

Soul Rest 1

Day 1: Cease From Your Own Work 2
Day 2: Come to Jesus 4
Day 3: Take His Yoke 6
Day 4: Learn from Him 8
Day 5: Let Go 10
Day 6: Walk with Jesus 12
Day 7: Pause and Reflect 17

Spirit Rest 19

Day 8: Rest in God's Forgiveness 20
Day 9: Find Rest in Forgiving Others 22
Day 10: Rest in Jesus' Victory and Authority 24
Day 11: Rest in Jesus' Freedom......................................26
Day 12: Rest in God's Power to Transform You 28
Day 13: The Holy Spirit 30
Day 14: Pause and Reflect..34

Mind Rest 35

Day 15: A Still Mind...36
Day 16: An Uncluttered Mind 38
Day 17: A Steadfast Mind..40
Day 18: A Renewed Mind 42
Day 19: A Spirit-led Mind 44
Day 20: Abiding – Keeping Your Mind at Rest 46
Day 21: Pause and Reflect...50

Body Rest 51

Day 22: Stillness 52
Day 23: Balance 54
Day 24: Rest in Nature...56
Day 25: Rest Through Nourishment..........................58
Day 26: Rest in Our Work..60
Day 27: Sabbath...62
Day 28: Pause and Reflect...66

Places of Rest... 67

Day 29: Rest in His Body..68
Day 30: Rest in His Boundaries 70

Some Final Thoughts..72
Steps in Forgiveness...76
How to Know Jesus 78

Welcome

Hello, beautiful mother, and welcome to your 30-day journey with God. As you read this devotional, I pray God plants His Word deep in your heart, adds new layers to your understanding and leads you into a greater experience of rest than you've ever known.

Twelve years ago, when I was busy in ministry and mothering four children, I hit a season of burnout. Overnight, I crumbled—physically, mentally and emotionally. The most basic tasks became overwhelming and fear was a daily companion. When I searched for encouragement in my well-worn bible, I couldn't understand the words. Desperate, I lifted a cry to God and wondered how—or if—I could ever recover.

God met me in my mess. Slowly and gently, He helped me break out of patterns of stress and striving, quieted my heart and led me into His rest. I discovered Jesus' work on the cross really had made the way for me to be welcomed and loved by Him, even when I didn't accomplish anything significant. Over several months I learned a new way of living and my strength gradually returned. When I returned to normal life,

I did so with a new sense of God's presence and a determination to stay in His rest.

This rest has become my lifelong pursuit. I'm a fallible woman, prone to fretting, and I know the only way I can dwell in God's rest is to keep meditating on His truth. I've spent thousands of hours poring over my Bible and asking God to grow me as a woman of rest. Now, it's my joy to share the principles I've been learning with you.

You'll notice the devotions are divided into weekly themes—Rest of Soul, Spirit, Mind and Body, with two final devotions on Rest in Your Place. The sixth devotion each week delves deeper into the current theme, so you may need a little more time to read those. I've included a question at the end of each devotion to help you travel beyond head knowledge to a tangible experience of God's rest. Please take time to reflect and act on them. God is ready to move in your life—if you'll give Him space to do so.

Bless you, lovely one. Enjoy the journey.

Warmly,

Sue

DAY 1:

Cease From Your Own Work

'... anyone who enters God's rest also rests from their own works, just as God did from his.'
Hebrews 4:10

This is where the journey begins. Sabbath rest is found when you rest from your own work.

'What does that mean?' you ask. 'I can't spend all day resting. I've got tasks to do, people to take care of.'

Yes, you do. Your life can be very busy. These words aren't talking about stopping physical work. They're not even talking about a once-a-week day off, though a weekly Sabbath is vital. To rest from your work is to lay down your striving and enter God's Sabbath rest—a *permanent* state of repose or perfect calm in your soul, that inner place where your mind, will and emotions reside.

Every day, you're bombarded by voices telling you it's all up to you. They say you need to strive and push to hold everything together, to prove yourself—as a woman, a wife, a mum and more. And if you blow it, you'll need to work extra hard to make up for your failings.

These voices are lying. God isn't cracking the whip, telling you to work harder. He's calling you to come, to lay down your drive to perform and enter His rest through faith in Jesus. The moment before He died on the cross Jesus said, 'It is finished.' His work was complete. By offering Himself as a sacrifice, He paid the price for your forgiveness and cleansing, opening the way for you to run into God's arms—wholly accepted. Jesus' work was perfect. You don't need to add to it.[1]

Ephesians 2:8-9 says, 'For it is by grace you have been saved, through faith—and this not from yourselves, it is the gift of God—not by works, so that no one can boast.'

This welcome into God's rest is a gift—not something you have to earn. Just receive it with thanks. And feel His loving arms embrace you, bringing perfect calm to your soul.

In what way have you been striving?

Are you ready to lay it down?

---

[1] For further understanding, please read 'How to Know Jesus' on p. 78

DAY 2:

Come to Jesus

*'Come to me, all you who are weary and
burdened, and I will give you rest.'*
Matthew 11:28

Jesus sees you, precious mother. He knows your weariness. He sees every choice you make to give to your family—even when you don't feel like it, even when no one else sees or appreciates your effort. He understands the tug-of-war between your desire to give your best to your loved ones and your longing to just curl up and sleep for a week. And He's calling you to come to Him, to seek rest in His presence.

He knows about your burden, that heavy yoke[2] you've been wearing that's enslaving you, weighing you down and wearing you out.

---

[2] A yoke is a wooden cross piece that is fastened over the necks of two animals and attached to the plough or cart that they are to pull
(https://www.google.com/search?q=yoke+definition&rlz=
1C1JZAP_enAU835AU835&oq=yoke+definition&aqs= chrome..
69i57j0i512l2j0i20i263i512j0i512l6. 4010j1j7&sourceid
=chrome&ie=UTF-8)

Maybe it's the dream wife yoke,

the super-mum yoke,

the successful career woman yoke,

or the perfectly put-together and always beautiful yoke.

For me, the dream wife and super-mum yokes had me striving to meet some crazy ideals then sinking into despair every time I failed. Whatever yoke you've taken on, Jesus is crying out, *'Come to Me! Come with that burden you were never meant to bear and let me remove it from your neck. Feel the relief to your aching shoulders as I lift the load from you.'* (See Isaiah 10:27)

Jesus' heart is not for you to drag your feet through your days, weary and burdened with unnecessary weight. He offers you rest—at every moment.

Are you carrying a false burden?

Bring it before the LORD and let Him lift it from your shoulders.

He has a better way for you.

DAY 3:

Take His Yoke

'Take my yoke upon you...'
Matthew 11:29

'What?' I hear you say. 'I thought Jesus wanted to take our burdens. Now He wants to put a yoke on us? How can wearing a yoke of any kind give us rest?'

For now, know this: Jesus' yoke is unlike any other.

In traditional agriculture, a good farmer takes time to shape each yoke so it fits the size and shape of the bearer. With careful hands, he carves and smooths the timber so it won't rub or cause pain. With a well-fitting yoke, his livestock can move with greater ease, almost as if they aren't wearing a yoke at all.

Can you see the parallel? Jesus knows you intimately—how you're 'shaped', inside and out. In fact, He shaped you perfectly for His purposes. And He knows just how to make His yoke fit you well so, rather than cause pain (as false yokes do), it enables you to live the life He planned. We'll talk more about this tomorrow.

A few years ago, God spoke these powerful words to me:

'Yieldedness is the place of rest.'

As I sensed His words I saw a mental image of an ox bowing its head to take on its master's yoke. In the same way, we need to bow before Jesus. When He tells you to take on His yoke He's asking you to surrender—to give up your right to be in control—and submit to His way. He's asking you to trust Him, to yield rather than wrestle.

Many times, I've wrestled with God because I couldn't see His purpose in my circumstances or I was afraid to walk the path He had for me. That wrestling didn't fix anything, it just made me anxious, angry and miserable. When I finally yielded, peace came. Calm came. Rest returned and, once again, I could hear God's voice and sense His direction for the way forward.

Are you wrestling with God over something?

In what area is He asking you to surrender to Him?

DAY 4:

Learn from Him

'Take my yoke upon you and learn from Me, for I am gentle and humble in heart, and you will find rest for your souls.'
Matthew 11:29

In some countries, yokes are still used in agriculture. When a young ox is introduced to farm work, it is yoked together with a strong, older animal. The farmer watches closely as they begin walking side by side, the mature ox setting the pace and direction and the little ox learning to walk in step. The young animal doesn't need to figure out what to do—it just has to match its stride with that of its elder. It has one job to do: stay in step with the big guy.

When Jesus asks you to take on His yoke, He's not expecting you to set out on your own and try to figure out the way as you go. Every day He'll be right beside you in the yoke, ready to show you the best route to take—if you're willing to learn.

To learn from Jesus, beautiful one, you need to grow in knowing Him. You can do this by reading His Word, listening to His voice and becoming familiar with His character through the Holy Spirit.

Sometimes it's difficult to hear what Jesus is saying. Your mind can be full of so many voices, it seems impossible to know which one is His. We'll cover more on listening soon. In the meantime, Matthew 11 offers an important tip: Jesus is gentle and humble in heart. He's not harsh or condemning. If the voice you're hearing stirs up striving, pride, anxiety, or brings a sense of condemnation, it's not Jesus.

His voice brings rest to your soul that surpasses any other.

What's one barrier that stops you learning from Jesus?

How can you remove it?

DAY 5:

Let Go

'Take my yoke upon you and learn from Me, for I am gentle and humble in heart, and you will find rest for your souls. For My yoke is easy and My burden is light.'
Matthew 11:29-30

How can a yoke be easy? And a burden light?

When a farmer yokes a young ox to a mature one, he fastens the yoke in such a way that the big ox's shoulders bear most of the load. The little ox is free to trot lightly along, oblivious to the fact that the strong one beside it is carrying all the weight.

This is a valuable principle for mothers just like you. Some days in your hectic, unpredictable world—even when you're seeking to walk with Jesus—weariness and overwhelm can press so heavy upon you that you wonder whether you can go on. Jesus is ready to bear your burdens.

Psalm 68:19 says, 'Praise be to the Lord, to God our Saviour, who daily bears our burdens.' Jesus doesn't *remove* the hard times from your days. He removes the *strain* of them, lifting the weight from your weary shoulders and giving you hope, courage and His strategies for the way forward.

There's an old saying, 'A burden shared is a burden halved.' In this case, a burden shared with Jesus is a burden lifted. The yoke He offers you is easy and His burden is light because He bears the weight of both of these for you—if you hand them over.

1 Peter 5:7 says, 'Cast all your anxiety on him because he cares for you.' Jesus is right beside you in the yoke, fully aware of your need and ready to bring relief. All you need to do is let go. When you do, like the young ox, you'll be able to walk with a lighter step *and* a lighter heart, knowing the strong one is shouldering your burdens on your behalf.

What cares have you been carrying?

Cast them on to Jesus and leave them with Him.

DAY 6:

Walk with Jesus

'My sheep listen to my voice; I know them, and they follow me.'
John 10:27

In 2010, my life was humming along—a jam-packed, fulfilling mix of home-schooling, leading women's ministry at church and dabbling in some creative projects. Partway through the year, God led us to make two drastic changes: to enrol our children in school and to see my husband apply for a political lobbyist position—trading his routine science position for a role laden with stress and conflict.

In just a few weeks, my whole concept of who we were as a family changed. My mind ran wild with thoughts of all the challenges ahead for everyone and I took on the burden of responsibility for them all—a load far too big for my shoulders. It wasn't long before I crumbled, utterly exhausted. The most basic tasks exhausted me and minor, everyday problems sparked heart flutters and chest pains. I dragged myself around the house, my mind so clouded with fog that it was difficult to read, think or make everyday decisions.

Burnout, they called it. To me, it felt more like death.

On the day everyone headed off to their new ventures, I flumped onto the couch with our toddler, drowning in loss and confusion. How was I supposed to live this new life? Not only had I 'lost' most of my family, I wasn't well enough to continue my ministry to women. I felt useless, stripped back to bare bones. What value did I have to God if I couldn't do anything significant? Who was I and where did I now fit into His plan?

Slowly, over the weeks that followed, He opened my eyes. What I'd been viewing as a disaster was in fact a gift—an opportunity to return to my first love. It was just me and God. No titles. No special roles. No need for me to achieve or perform.

I fed my ailing spirit with simple Bible teaching and worship music, and filled countless journal pages with my rambling thoughts. Little by little, my mind began to clear. I sensed God's whisper, repeatedly assuring me of His constant love—even on my 'laziest' days. I didn't need to perform to earn His approval. What He most wanted me to do at that time was rest.

When I asked for prayer one Sunday after church, our pastor, a dear friend, spent time in silent prayer before saying:

'Sue, you're a very strong person and I know this time of weakness is difficult. I believe God wants to bring you to a new place in your relationship with Him, where you live out of *His* strength rather than relying on your own.'

My weary heart flickered with hope. And desire. After tasting the sweetness of God's rest, I didn't want to go back to who I'd been before.

Lord, thank You. Please show me Your way. Teach me how to walk with You.

Ever since that day, God has been answering that prayer, teaching me vital principles of walking with Him. I'd love to share them with you.

1. Know who you are in God.

    Though He is the Almighty Creator who reigns far above everything in your world, He's inviting you to come and rest in His embrace. Let Him sing over you, quieting your anxious heart. (Zephaniah 3:17). He says, *'You are my daughter, my darling, my treasured possession. I will never let you go.'*

    (Read Zephaniah 3:17, Deuteronomy 7:6, John 10:28)

2. Rely on Jesus.

    The yoke Jesus has crafted for you makes it easy for you to walk in step with Him. As you yield to His yoke and rely on Him to take the weight of the load, it will feel lighter than you expect. No matter how difficult the path ahead may be, Jesus will walk every step with you, showing you where to place your foot.

(Matthew 11:28-29, Galatians 5:1)

3. Seek constant connection with Jesus.

   Jesus—not your titles or achievements—is your source of life. Maintain a strong connection with Him. Feed on His Word and slow down to listen for His voice. Then you will thrive. No good fruit can come from your own striving.

   (John 3:6, 15: 4-8)

4. Trust God's timing.

   When setbacks come, remember your times are in God's hands. You can trust His timing. Don't try to push ahead of Him *or* to resist His leading. His eye is always on you and He will unfold His purposes at just the right pace.

   (Psalm 31:14-15)

5. Tune in to the Holy Spirit.

   When you surrendered your life to God, He gave you His Holy Spirit to comfort and lead you and enable you to walk with Him (John

14:16-17). We'll talk more about the Spirit in the days ahead. For now, ask God to make you aware of His little nudges throughout your days. If you follow those nudges, you'll see just how much God wants to be involved in your life.

(Psalm 23:6, Galatians 5:25)

Which principle of walking with Jesus do you sense God highlighting for you at this time?

DAY 7:
Pause and Reflect

How has your understanding of rest grown this week?

Do you view your relationship with Jesus differently?

Open your heart to receive all God wants to impart to you over the weeks to come.

*'In repentance and rest is your salvation,
in quietness and trust is your strength . . .'*

Isaiah 30: 15b

DAY 8:

Rest in God's Forgiveness

'This is my blood of the covenant, which is poured out for many for the forgiveness of sins.'
Matthew 26:28

How many times has guilt over your failings as a mum kept you from experiencing God's rest? You know Jesus gave His life to pay for your forgiveness. But somehow you feel like that wasn't enough.

Maybe you lost your temper and, in the intensity of the moment, said or did things you knew were hurtful. Maybe you were slow to respond to your child's needs for the umpteenth time that day. Maybe you vented your thoughts like a free-flowing stream on someone who couldn't deal with them. Or you got so busy, you forgot to do a job you were supposed to prioritise.

Did you feel the 'perfect mother yoke' grip you like a straitjacket that day, squeezing all hope from your heart and convincing you that you're a disappointment to God?

Remember, daughter of the Lord, Satan is the master liar and accuser. His whole mission is to sideline you, to keep you from the One who is both able and ready to restore you. The devil pulls out all his favourite weapons, hissing in your ear, '*No one* else struggles like this. You're the *only* one. You're *always* going to be a terrible mother. You'll *never* break free of this struggle.' His voice is nasty, his tone convincing. So you hide, filling your days with activity and noise to avoid facing the guilt and despair in your heart.

All the while, Jesus is saying, *'Come! You don't need to hide. I know you. I love you. And I want to restore you. Just come. Bring your sin into My light and let me wash you clean. Nothing is too big or too awful for Me to forgive and cleanse. Come! Receive forgiveness. Come and let your spirit be at rest. The Father is waiting for you and His arms are open wide.'*

Are you still carrying guilt and shame for some sin? Bring it to Jesus and receive His forgiveness and cleansing.

DAY 9:

Find Rest in Forgiving Others

'And forgive us our sins, as we have forgiven those who have sinned against us.'
Matthew 6:12
(International Standard Version)

'Don't take the bait.' I was standing beside my husband in church, seething over something he'd just done. His actions weren't serious but to me on that day, they seemed like a major crime. Then God's whisper came.

The devil was out to trap me with his bait of offence. It was he who kept mental replays of the 'crime' rolling in my mind. All he wanted was to entangle me in bitterness and take my eyes off God.

Offence steals our rest, bringing agitation and *unrest*. It undermines our relationships—especially with God. In Matthew 6, Jesus said God forgives us *as we have* forgiven. Soon after, He added, '. . . with the measure you use, it will be measured to you.' (Matthew 7:1-2)

God's love for us is unconditional but His forgiveness has firm conditions. If we want to be released from judgement for our sin, we need to release others from *our* judgement for *their* sin. If we're merciful, God will show us mercy. But if we deal with people harshly—even in our mind—God promises to deal harshly with us.

When you become a mum, you climb aboard one crazy lifelong roller-coaster ride. From the soaring joy you feel at the birth of your baby, through the plummet into panic when you can't settle them, to the rattling uncertainty when everything seems out of control, you have a lot of emotions to juggle. Add in broken sleep, fluctuating hormones, limited couple time, reopened wounds from your own childhood and pure exhaustion, and you are left vulnerable—with many opportunities for hurt and offence.

Take a moment to remember the battle you're in. Your offence may seem justified but holding on to it will only do damage—to you and to others. Your enemy wants to suck you into a vortex of pain and isolation. God calls you to forgive and let go, by His enabling. When you lay down your offence, the enemy's hold in that area of your life will be broken and you will experience God's mercy and enjoy rest in your spirit once more.[3]

Who do you need to forgive today?

---

[3] For further understanding, see 'Steps in Forgiveness' on p. 76.

DAY 10:

Rest in Jesus' Victory and Authority

'And having disarmed the powers and authorities, he made a public spectacle of them, triumphing over them by the cross.'
Colossians 2:15

Do you ever feel like it's impossible to find victory in an area of your life? There is hope: Jesus has disarmed the devil and his crew, stripping them of all authority. Like a king of old who paraded his captives through the streets, when Jesus hung on the cross, He publicly disgraced those who had tried to conquer Him. What looked like defeat was in fact a mighty spiritual victory. And as His heirs, we now share in His triumph.

Beautiful mama, you may not feel victorious right now. Life can sometimes feel like a relentless battle. Still, in Christ you are a victor. Paul wrote, 'In all these things we are *more than conquerors* through him who loved us.' (Romans 8:37, emphasis mine)

More than conquerors, 'super-conquerors', winners of a surpassing victory. That's you. That's me. Whatever your stage of mum life, if you belong to Jesus, He has made you a mighty overcomer. His victory is available to you—over sickness, depression, confusion, fear and anything else your enemy would try to put on you. And just like your salvation, that victory is a gift to be received with thanks, not something you have to strive for.

Jesus lived in victory by walking in complete submission to the Father—even when the cost was intense. So it is with you. When you submit to God's rule in your life, He'll lead you into His spiritual victory—step by step.

I once went through a season of almost daily battles with a determined child. As I cried out to God, He said, '*If you humble yourself and obey Me, I'll intervene on your behalf. Submission is the place of authority.*' Rather than try to assert my own authority, He wanted me to rest in the security of His authority. As I chose to trust Him and follow His lead, dynamics with that child slowly began to change.

Jesus knows the best way for each of us to experience His victory. His way may not always make sense to us—sometimes it might even seem like defeat. But if we're willing to trust Him and obey, He will fight for us.

In what area is the Lord challenging you to submit to Him, so He can lead you to spiritual victory?

DAY 11:

Rest in Jesus' Freedom

'Then you will know the truth, and the truth will set you free ... So if the Son sets you free, you will be free indeed.'
John 8:32, 36

Don't you love the word 'freedom'? When I hear it, I always imagine someone running with arms outstretched in glorious sunshine—a vivid image of life with Jesus. Through His death and resurrection, He has released us from slavery to sin and to Satan, then washed us clean, forgiven us and ushered us into God's family—wholly accepted.

To know the truth in this verse is much more than merely having head knowledge. It's knowing Jesus—*the* truth—that will set you free. The freedom Jesus offers won't fluctuate with your emotions or performance. It's been bought with His precious blood. When Jesus sets you free you are truly, wonderfully free—indeed!

Learning to live in that freedom is a lifelong process, beginning in your mind. The enemy will do all he can to keep you in the mindset of a slave. He'll try to manipulate you through other people's expectations. Haunt you with trauma from your past. Lure you into destructive habit patterns. And convince you that true freedom is out-of-reach. What a liar!

Satan no longer has the right to rule you. He's been thoroughly defeated by Jesus. Still, he tries—tempting you to agree with his lies, hide your wounds and wander down his dark alleys of temptation. To renew your mind, you need to regularly feed on the truth. Then, the Holy Spirit will show you His way of escape from the enemy's snares.

Precious woman, Jesus has removed your chains and led you into God's family. Through faith in Him, you are now a royal daughter—God's treasured possession. You have permission to walk tall and free, secure in the knowledge of the Father's total acceptance of you. You're free to live with a strong sense of value and purpose. And you can be confident that God will provide all you need to fulfil His purpose—and continue to grow in the spirit rest His freedom brings.

In what ways are you still thinking like a slave?

Meditate on the freedom Jesus bought for you and ask the Holy Spirit to teach you how to walk in His freedom, step by step.

DAY 12:

Rest in God's Power to Transform You

'Therefore, if anyone is in Christ, the new creation has come: the old has gone, the new is here!'
2 Corinthians 5:17

When you surrendered your life to Jesus, a miracle happened. Just like the first day of creation when God—with a word—introduced light to a world bathed in darkness, the moment you were saved He breathed life into your spirit by His Spirit. While this inner transformation was immediate, seeing its reality outworked in your life takes time.

In each person, God's process of transformation is unique. You may go through times when you sense Him putting His finger on an area you'd rather He didn't touch. You shrink back, afraid the pain and mess of the change process will overwhelm you. Conversely, you might be fed up with an area of weakness in your character and desperate to see change—fast.

Whichever way you're tempted to take control, remember this: it's not up to you to direct the course or the pace of your transformation. God knows you. He loves you. He knows the best way for you to experience change that lasts. And He's inviting you to partner with Him.

In Philippians 2:12-13, Paul wrote about 'working out' our salvation. This implies we need to apply effort to align our lives with our new spirit. Yet, he goes on to say that it is *God* who works in us to bring that change and it is Him who empowers us to fulfil His purposes. You don't have to transform yourself—just cooperate with God.

There will be times when God leads you to take practical action—to receive prayer, renew your mind with the Word or even be equipped by others to develop new habits. All these steps are valuable on the journey. But God directs the overall process. And you can rest confident that as you trust and submit to Him, change will come. He who began a good work in you will be faithful to complete it (Philippians 1:6).

Who are you relying on to transform you?

Release to God any area where you're trying to transform yourself rather than resting in Him.

DAY 13:
The Holy Spirit

This week you've been journeying into spirit rest, which is only possible with the enabling of God's Holy Spirit. When you surrender yourself to Jesus, the Holy Spirit comes to dwell in your spirit, bringing new life. He enables you to receive God's forgiveness and cleansing, and gives you the grace to forgive those who have hurt you. The Spirit leads you into ever-increasing freedom and authority. He transforms you from the inside out.

What do you think of when you hear mention of the Holy Spirit? An unseen force? A mystic being? You may know He is a member of the Trinity, equal in divine status to the Father and Jesus. But who is He? It can be difficult to grasp His nature with our limited human understanding. Here are a few thoughts from the Word that are relevant to us as mothers.

1. Breath of God

    In Zechariah 4:6, God said to Zerubbabel, 'Not by might nor by power, but by my Spirit.' The word God used for spirit here meant 'breath' or 'wind'. It was by the breath of God that Zerubbabel was able to complete the huge, seemingly insurmountable task of rebuilding the temple.

What tasks are you facing that seem too hard or too huge? With God's breath fuelling you, even towering mountains can suddenly seem scalable. If you're willing to look beyond your own limitations to the boundless power of the Holy Spirit, you'll see things that appeared impossible become possible.

2. Giver of victory

   The Holy Spirit raised Jesus from the dead. Romans 8:11 says you now have that same Spirit living in you, giving supernatural life and victory—even and especially when you feel utterly weak and inadequate. God's Spirit is more than able to fill your gaps and make up for your failings.

   Doesn't this bring a great sigh of relief? God doesn't need your oomph for His plan to be worked out in your life. He simply asks you to walk with Him—to live dependent. He has anointed you with His Holy Spirit so you can know the truth and walk in it (1 John 2:20).

3. Counsellor

   In John 14, Jesus calls the Holy Spirit 'the advocate'—the one who walks alongside as comforter and counsellor. This is what I appreciate most about the Spirit's presence in my life. Daily, I'm revived by His support and encouragement. Daily, I seek His guidance to keep me on the right path—both in thought and action.

   God's Spirit is the Spirit of truth, who leads us in the ways of Jesus. He will never lead us astray (John 16:13-14)

4. Wind

   In John 3:8, Jesus spoke of the Holy Spirit as a wind that, 'blows wherever it pleases.' We can't contain or control the Spirit of God. To follow His guidance, you need to let go of control and be willing to go wherever He directs. You can be sure His leading will always line up with God's plan.

God's Holy Spirit reveals the nature of God to us. He is breath. He is power. He is comfort and counsel. And He is the ultimate truth-speaker. The more you rely on Him to lead and enable you, the more satisfying and rich your life will become. Even as you launch out onto unfamiliar paths, He will walk beside you, bringing reassurance and rest to the depths of your spirit.

Are you willing to allow the Holy Spirit to work in your life and lead you in God's ways?

As you surrender control, be alert to His presence, giving you strength, direction and rest.

DAY 14:

Pause and Reflect

What key thoughts from this week were new to you?

Record them somehow—write in a journal, attach them to the mirror or wall.

Meditate on them by reading what you've written or playing songs with related lyrics and allow God to bring new understanding and rest to your spirit.

DAY 15:

A Still Mind

'Be still, and know that I am God; I will be exalted among the nations, I will be exalted in the earth.'
Psalm 46:10

Being still requires you to cease striving and 'hang limp', sinking into a relaxed posture of waiting. It also means quieting the noise in your head—which sometimes causes more unrest than any outward busyness. When you slow down and fix your thoughts on God, two important truths become clear:

1. He is God.

2. You are not.

God is the mighty creator—maker of heaven and earth—who watches over His creation, sustaining every part. He reigns on high, far above everything that's going on in your life. And, treasured daughter, He has chosen to be *your* God and walk with you through each day. Amazing!

There are seasons in mum-life where being still can seem impossible. When I was in that stage with our children I resorted to snatching little moments of pause—when I was lying in bed in the morning or evening, while I used the shower or toilet, drove somewhere or watched our children play. Or in the hallowed quiet of naptime.

If you find it difficult to pull your thoughts away from all the tasks on your to-do list, you might like to try using worship music, visual reminders or memory verses to centre your thoughts on God. Ask Him to help you find a creative way to restore your focus and try to develop a new habit. The more often you can still your mind and remember God is with you, reigning over all that concerns you, the more you'll experience rest in His strong, reassuring presence.

When you take time to be still and focus on God today, what attribute does He highlight to you?

Find a way to meditate on that reality and let it shift your perspective.

DAY 16:

An Uncluttered Mind

'"Martha, Martha," the Lord answered, "you are worried and upset about many things, but few things are needed—or indeed only one. Mary has chosen what is better, and it will not be taken away from her."'
Luke 10: 41-42

Martha was on the verge of a breakdown. Jesus could see she was divided into many parts by her multitude of thoughts—she was mentally 'going to pieces.' Her mind was in such a state of overwhelm that her thoughts gushed out at her special guest in an angry outburst.

Doesn't that remind you of days we face as mums—those times life feels so chaotic it's difficult to manage a deep breath, let alone a sustained train of thought? Sometimes the mayhem comes from sources beyond our control. Sometimes it stems from our choices to set unrealistic goals or overload our schedule.

Jesus' response to Martha was simple and direct. She needed to still her frantic mind and focus on the one thing she truly needed—His presence. It's the same with you and me. Our mind can be cluttered with a thousand whirring thoughts. Jesus wants us to lay them all at His feet and let Him sift them, weeding out the rubbish and leaving what brings life.

God has not given you a spirit of fear but of love, power and a sound—or self-controlled—mind (New King James Version, 2 Timothy 1:7). By His Spirit, you have the power to choose which thoughts you allow into your mind. You can listen to the enemy's whispers of doubt and panic or fill your mind with the truth of God's power and goodness. When you declutter and refocus your mind, your vision will clear and rest will return.

Ask God to show you one way you can declutter your life and mind.

There may be an extra activity, an unrealistic expectation or a project you've tried to squeeze in where it doesn't fit.

Trust God to show you what to keep and what to lay down. He loves you!

DAY 17:

A Steadfast Mind

'You will keep in perfect peace those whose minds are steadfast, because they trust in you.'
Isaiah 26:3

I was given this verse the day I graduated from bible college—probably because of the ways I had battled anxiety during my time there. Many times since graduation day, I've mulled over these words, hungry for the perfect peace they promise.

I always imagined that being steadfast meant gritting my teeth and standing firm with all my might. When I researched its true meaning in a lexicon, I was surprised to discover it means to lean upon or take hold of, to lay, rest, support and be braced. Did you see that? To '*be* braced', not to brace ourselves. This dynamic isn't dependent on our strength—it relies on the strength of the One we lean on.

When you find your security in God's love and goodness and lean on Him as your firm foundation, He'll keep your mind in a place of perfect peace. Once again, it's *Him* who keeps your mind in that state. All you need to do is trust.

The word used for both perfect and peace in this promise is 'shalom', which means completeness, soundness, welfare, wholeness, a sense that all is well. Having this word repeated—'shalom shalom'—implies you'll be given an extra generous measure of peace and wholeness as you lean wholeheartedly on God. What a promise!

In the same way, Proverbs 3:5-6 urges you to trust God with your whole heart. It warns against leaning on your own, often shaky, understanding. Dear sister, you can lean hard on God, trusting Him to take the full weight of your load, and look to Him to lead you. When you do, He'll direct your steps on the way that is straight, smooth and right.

Ask God to show you what you're leaning on.

Is it a firm foundation?

DAY 18:

A Renewed Mind

'Therefore, I urge you ... to offer your bodies as a living sacrifice ... Do not conform to the pattern of this world, but be transformed by the renewing of your mind. Then you will be able to test and approve what God's will is—his good, pleasing and perfect will.'
Romans 12:1-2

When you offer yourself to God, this includes surrendering your mind to Him. While He instantly brings a complete renewal in your spirit (as discussed on Day 12), the renewal of your mind happens more gradually.

Just like any building renovation, God's plan is to remove your old, dead ways of thinking and replace them with fresh, life-giving truth. Paul writes, '*be transformed*', hinting that you have an active part to play in the mind renovation process.

Here are some practical steps you can take to change the way you think:

- place verses and quotes in prominent positions around your home
- read the word aloud, declaring and praying truth
- listen to teaching on topics of interest or need
- listen and sing along to music that is rich in truth
- receive ministry to deal with causes of distorted thinking
- have close friends or mentors who are willing to challenge and speak truth to you

As you align your mind more closely with God's Word, you'll find it easier to sense and understand His will, even as you go about your day with its multitude of decisions.

What is one step you can take now to help renew your mind?

DAY 19:

A Spirit-led Mind

'Those who live according to the flesh have their minds set on what the flesh desires; but those who live in accordance with the Spirit have their minds set on what the Spirit desires. The mind governed by the flesh is death, but the mind governed by the Spirit is life and peace.'
Romans 8:5-6

Whatever you set your mind on will govern your thoughts and direct your behaviour. Whatever you devote yourself to will dictate the way you live. You can follow your fleshly desires, which fluctuate day to day, or eagerly pursue God's perspective and direction.

In the above passage, the word Paul used for the Holy Spirit also referred to wind—something powerful and beyond human control. Your enemy is bent on keeping you from following the Spirit's leading, so he sows seeds of doubt and fear into your mind, making you question the 'safety' of living in God's ways. To listen to the devil and let your emotions direct your choices is to choose death—both physical and spiritual.

Further on, in Romans 8, Paul reminds his readers they're not slaves pushed around by a frightening taskmaster, but sons of God. As are you, through faith in Jesus. There is no need to fear. Your Father God has invited you to dwell in His house, to find rest in His loving embrace and freely dip into His lavish resources.

My friend, lay down your fear, let go of control and set your mind on what the Holy Spirit says. Then you'll experience a new level of the life, rest and peace God has for you to enjoy.

What is one area of your thinking where you're not enjoying life, rest and peace?

Reflect on God's deep love for you, surrender your mind to the Holy Spirit's rule and allow Him to lead you in a new, life-giving way of thinking.

DAY 20:

Abiding – Keeping Your Mind at Rest

"'I am the vine; you are the branches. If you remain in me and I in you, you will bear much fruit; apart from me you can do nothing. If you do not remain in me, you are like a branch that is thrown away and withers; such branches are picked up, thrown into the fire and burned. If you remain in me and my words remain in you, ask whatever you wish, and it will be done for you. This is to my Father's glory, that you bear much fruit, showing yourselves to be my disciples.'"
John 15: 5-8

Beautiful one, Jesus invites you to *dwell* with Him, not visit sporadically. He is the true vine—your source of life and nourishment. To live well, you need to remain closely connected to Him. Like a branch that relies on the vine, if you detach from Him, you'll wither. The older I get, the more clearly I see the truth of these words, 'Apart from Me you can do nothing.' Without Jesus, I really am lost—incapable of living a good life. But when I abide with Him, anything is possible.

Have you noticed how branches on a grapevine never labour to bear fruit? All they do is hang upon the trellis, waiting for nourishment to flow from the root and make them flourish. As long as they're connected to a healthy vine, fruit will surely come. In the same way, we don't need to strive to thrive. We just need to stay connected to Jesus. He's the one who supplies what we need for a fruitful life.

Psalm 91:1 says, 'Whoever dwells in the shelter of the Most High will rest in the shadow of the Almighty.' Did you notice the key words in this promise: 'dwell' and 'rest'? Their meanings are similar. The word used here for rest means lodge, remain with, hang all night. And dwell means to sit or remain. When we 'hang with Jesus', He gives us rest in His shelter.

One morning last year I felt God say:

'I don't want My people to live for *Me. I want them to live* with *Me.'*

More than your works or performance, Jesus is after *you*—your heart, your mind, your trust and your devotion. He calls you to live with Him so you can find rest in His presence, feel His heartbeat and bear so much fruit that people who taste it are drawn to His goodness. (John 15:7-8)

So how do you abide?

1. Acknowledge your need

   For all of us, abiding begins at the same point—acknowledging how desperately we need Jesus and how utterly lost we are without Him. The more you draw near to Him in prayer, the more confident you'll grow in the constancy of His presence with you.

2. Feed on the Word

   Taking time to read the Word helps build understanding of God's ways and His heart. Read regularly. Read often. Read big chunks. Spend long periods studying tiny portions. Meditate on the Living Word and let it transform the way you live. The more you taste its goodness, the hungrier you'll be for more.

   (Psalm 119: 11, 105, Hebrews 4:12).

3. Rely on the Holy Spirit

   God has given you His Holy Spirit to enable you to walk with Jesus and show others His goodness (Acts 1:8). The Spirit is your counsellor and guide, the One who gives you power to live a life that goes far beyond what comes naturally.

   (Psalm 16:7-8, Psalm 32:8, Isaiah 30:21, Ephesians 3:20, 2 Peter 1:3)

Through the years, I've met people who demonstrated such peace, wisdom and quiet strength, they stirred in me a hunger to know Jesus as they did. It led me to take more time to pray, to study the Word and grow in sensitivity to the Holy Spirit. Now, my intimacy with the Lord is my greatest joy, and I know there's still so much more of Him to discover.

Here's a wonderful promise for us all:

"'You will seek me and find me when you seek me with all your heart. I will be found by you," declares the LORD, "and will bring you back from captivity."' (Jeremiah 29:13-14a)

What is one practical step you can take to grow in your connection to Jesus?

DAY 21:
Pause and Reflect

How has your understanding changed regarding your mind this week?

Which principle was most significant to you?

Ask God to show you how to apply what you've learned so you can grow in mind rest.

DAY 22:

Stillness

'The LORD is my shepherd, I lack nothing.
He makes me lie down in green pastures,
he leads me beside quiet waters,
he refreshes my soul.'
Psalm 23:1-3a

I remember it well—the weariness of the early years as a mum. That wading-through-soup heaviness, the fatigue and nausea that roll over you in waves, the groan of your body as you lower yourself into bed. Whatever stage of mum life you're in, if you're buckling under exhaustion, let me offer some encouragement. Jesus sees you. He understands how you feel and He's ready to bring refreshing and restoration. The words above say He *makes you* lie down. Did you notice that? Jesus is not a harsh slave driver, cracking the whip and telling you to work harder. Like a good shepherd with his sheep, He knows your need of time to lie down, stretch out and give yourself to total relaxation.

From the beginning of time, our Creator has been beckoning us to stillness. On the seventh day of creation, He rested, modelling Sabbath for all generations. He designed our bodies to fall asleep, even involuntarily, within every twenty-four hour period. He urged His people to be still (Psalm 46:10). To cease striving. To stop rushing around trying to tick all the boxes. And today, He gives you permission—more than that, a command—to stop. Even when you have unfinished tasks on your to-do list.

Proverbs 3:24 says people who walk in God's wisdom enjoy sleep that is peaceful and sweet—blissfully so. Sound good? Such true, total body rest comes only when you put your trust firmly in God. When you believe He'll make sure everything that needs to be done will be done—and anything that's left undone either isn't urgent or isn't necessary.

Your Father sees your life clearly and He knows all the tasks that weigh heavy on you. Today, let Him sift your to-do list, filtering out the excess, so you can enjoy being still in His presence. That is the place of rest and refreshing—body and soul.

What does stillness look like for you?

How can you plan stillness into your day?

DAY 23:

Balance

'There is a time for everything, and a season for every activity under the heavens...'
Ecclesiastes 3:1

God has infused all of creation with rhythm and balance. We see it in day and night, the moon's recurring phases, seedtime and harvest and the cycle of the seasons. Likewise, *you* were made to live with rhythm and balance in your physical activities. Solomon hinted at this in his lengthy, 'A time to...' reflection. Everything has its time and season, he wrote. Always, there is flux and movement.

God has gifted you with the capacity to do many things, yet He doesn't want you to engage in any of them excessively. Like a healthy tree that needs the right mix of sunshine, rain and nourishment from the soil, you'll bear the most fruit when you live with a healthy physical balance.

In that hectic, beautiful season when your children are young, your time use is mostly dictated by their needs. As years pass and your children grow more independent, your options grow and many choices lie before you. How can you arrange your days in a way that brings balance?

Here's a helpful principle: Extremes, even of good things, can throw your body out of balance and bring unrest. I remember a time when our boys were three and four years old, our daughter was a baby and we'd just begun home-schooling. I'd designed a quilt for our bed as an anniversary gift and was relishing short stints of creative time in my day. As each patchwork square took shape, my excitement grew and I gave more and more time to this project. Some nights I stayed up quilting so late, my husband went to bed alone and the next day my children bore the brunt of my tired crankiness.

Dear mother, if you notice yourself gravitating towards something in an out-of-balance way, stop and ask, 'Am I looking to this as my source of life and joy rather than to God?' It's a good time to reflect on your priorities and make some changes, as I did.

God alone knows the purpose He has for your life and what your future holds. As you seek to walk in rhythm with Him, you can trust He'll show you the best balance for now *and* prepare you for the seasons to come.

Is the Lord highlighting an area of imbalance in your life?

Lay it before Him and ask Him to show you His way into a healthier rhythm.

DAY 24:

Rest in Nature

'Now the LORD God had planted a garden in the east, in Eden; and there he put the man he had formed. The LORD God made all kinds of trees grow ... A river watering the garden flowed from Eden . .. the LORD God ... brought ... to the man (all the wild animals and all the birds in the sky) ...'
Genesis 2:8-10, 19

God takes great delight in His creation (Genesis 1:31, 3:8). It was His pleasure to settle the very first people in a lush, beautiful garden—rich in colour, movement and texture. All of nature has been infused with His life, so any time you spend immersed in it imparts life to you.

Time in nature restores your body. Your lungs inhale more oxygen, your mind clears, stress hormone levels plummet while feel-good ones rise, and your motivation and focus are sharpened. If you engage with nature in an active way—like bushwalking, climbing, swimming, surfing, horse-riding and more—your sense of wellbeing will multiply. Doesn't that make you want to head outdoors right now?

You may have noticed the slow, steady rhythm woven into the fabric of creation. It's in the roll and crash of waves at the beach, the gentle drift of clouds across the sky, the ripples of a stream over rocks—I'm sure you can think of more. These gentle, repetitive movements impact your body in a tangible way, slowing your heart rate and quieting your soul.

Then there are the details you see when you slow down long enough to look. The intricacies of a leaf, the sun faithfully rising each morning, the change in the air with each new season. When you sit atop a towering headland watching waves roar far below or gaze at the millions of stars in the night sky, you can't help but realise how very small you are—and how huge and mighty God is (Psalm 19:1, 93:4). This shift in perspective brings comfort and a new sense of confidence. If God is able to sustain all of creation through every season, He is more than able to sustain you.

You were made to be immersed in God's creation. What's one way you can build time in nature into your day?

DAY 25:

Rest Through Nourishment

'... no one ever hated their own body, but they feed and care for (it) ...'
Ephesians 5:29

Have you ever thought of your body as an instrument in God's hands? He often chooses to demonstrate His love to the people around you through your actions. Your ability to play your part in this dynamic will depend directly on how physically able you are to do the work He desires.

In the early chapters of Genesis, we read of the abundant food God created—colourful, delicious goodies, no doubt full of life-giving nutrients. Our generous Father made sure food was not only nourishing but beautiful—a pleasure to look at as well as to eat.

Today there are so many options in food and diet available to you, it can be a challenge to figure out the best way for your family—especially within your time and budget constraints. It's natural, as a busy mum, to opt for cheap, easy solutions or reach for food that brings comfort or boosts your energy. I've done the same and found that those quick fixes usually backfired. Highly processed foods and those laden with sugar and caffeine cause inflammation throughout your body, attacking your immune system, clouding your mind and sabotaging your sense of rest. Not only do they bring *you* down, they have the same negative impact on your children.

The closer a food is to its natural state—the way God made it—the more nourishment it provides. Good food helps your body heal and prevents you from getting ill. It provides sustained energy, helps stabilise your emotions and brings mental clarity.

When you're making food choices for yourself and your family, try to think beyond the moment. What do you want to reap over the next month? Year? Decade? On that basis, what do you need to sow into your body now?

God's way is always a way of peace, nurture and growth. When He corrects, He doesn't condemn you, rather He calls you to keep pressing forward, making adjustments as you go. As you ask Him for wisdom in this area, He'll show you His way for your family, one step at a time.

What is one change you can make to your eating habits to nourish your body and cultivate rest?

DAY 26:

Rest in Our Work

'The LORD God took the man and put him in the garden to work it and take care of it.'
Genesis 2:15

How do you view work? Do you see it as something you have to endure—an unwelcome burden of life in this fallen world? You may be surprised to read in the above verse that God assigned work to humanity *before* the world was tainted by sin. It was part of His perfect plan from the beginning.

In asking you to take on His yoke, Jesus is calling you both to walk with Him, and to do the work He assigns. For each of you, that work will be different. As Ephesians 2:10 says, 'we are God's handiwork, created in Christ Jesus to do good works, which God *prepared in advance* for us to do.' (emphasis mine)

Before you were even born, God had work planned for you, a part He wants you to play in His purposes for the world. Do you see what a privilege it is to co-labour with Him? As women, you've been created to reflect specific aspects of the image of God. When you work alongside Him in the power and leading of His Spirit, you demonstrate His nature to those around you—His loving rule, His creative wisdom, His nurturing heart, His faithfulness and so much more.

It's amazing the difference a shift in mindset can make. When you understand that you're part of a much bigger picture, even the most menial tasks can take on new significance. Suddenly, your work becomes worship—an offering of love.

Colossians 3:23-24 says, 'Whatever you do, work at it with all your heart, as working for the Lord, not for human masters . . . It is the Lord Christ you are serving.' Amen.

Ask the Lord to expose any false ideas about your work in this season and give you a fresh perspective.

DAY 27:

Sabbath

'Thus the heavens and the earth were completed in all their vast array. By the seventh day God had finished the work He had been doing; so on the seventh day He rested from all His work. Then God blessed the seventh day and made it holy, because on it He rested from all the work of creating that He had done.'
Genesis 2:1-3

Adam and Eve's first full day of life was a day of rest. Before their eyes, their Almighty Creator stopped working and took pleasure in slow time. God didn't need to rest—He never tires—but He chose to model it for His people because He knew they'd need rest as a regular practice. Here are some of the benefits of Sabbath rest.

1. A real break from work

    God created Sabbath for us—a day to cease, desist and stop all our usual work—both physically *and* mentally (think work texts, emails, social media posts and phone calls).

Sabbath is our opportunity to push aside all the busyness of our lives and rest in God's loving care. Mark Buchanan, author of *The Rest of God*,[4] says Sabbath rest is ceasing from what is necessary and doing that which brings life.

What does this look like for you—to cease from all the pressing tasks and do what revives you, inside and out? For each of us the answer will be different.

2. Renewal

   The word 'recreation' comes from its two parts, 're' and 'create'. It was originally used to refer to the curing of a sick person by the renewal of their body. God intends Sabbath to be a day of re-creation for us—a day of renewal, refreshing and healing—body, soul and spirit.

The bible college where my husband and I met made Sundays distinct and special. Duties were pared back, study was discouraged, hospitality was promoted and we were urged to slow down, trusting God to help us complete all our work the other six days of the week. What a gift those Sundays were! The rest of the college schedule was jam-packed, so we savoured every Sunday meal eaten at our leisure, every spontaneous group outing or afternoon relaxing on the lawn. We relished having time to talk deeply, to laugh, to reflect on all God was doing in our lives and to give thanks.

---

[4] Buchanan, M (2007). *The Rest of God.* Thomas Nelson Inc.

That day of rest each Sunday helped us rise on Monday morning with a lighter heart and a fresh spring in our step.

3. Investment in the week that follows

    Adam and Eve were blessed to experience rest *before* they began working in the garden (Genesis 2:15). This established Sabbath for them as a springboard into a fruitful, productive week, rather than a recovery day after six days of work. If we take this perspective, Sabbath begins to be viewed as an investment rather than a recovery period. We recognise the need to rest well in order to work well, not the other way around.

4. An opportunity to trust

    One final thought on this topic. God felt Sabbath was so important for godly living, He placed it fourth in His list of ten commandments (Exodus 20:8-11). If He puts such emphasis on Sabbath, the enemy will make it his mission to keep you from embracing it. He'll fire his flaming darts, pricking you with a burning sense of urgency about all the jobs you've tried to put aside. Or he'll tempt you to cram your day so full of activity, there's no time to truly slow down.

Precious sister, the devil is a hard taskmaster, always pushing you to go, go, go. God, on the other hand, is calling you to trust Him with all your tasks, to slow down the internal motor and let Him refresh you. Which will you choose?

What's one step you can take towards establishing a weekly day of rest?

DAY 28:
Pause and Reflect

How has your understanding of body rest changed in the last week?

Write down some small, practical steps you can take to experience greater rest in your body.

DAY 29:

Rest in His Body

'Now to each one the manifestation of the Spirit is given for the common good ... and he distributes them to each one, just as he determines.'
1 Corinthians 12:7, 11b

When God welcomed you into His family, He invited you to live in close connection with other believers. Just as the parts of a body work in sync, when God's people get together, all the gifts of His Spirit interact so everyone benefits.

There was nothing random about the way God allocated spiritual gifts to you. Before you were born, He determined the roles He wanted you to play in His purposes and He has gifted you with everything you need to fulfil them. Likewise, He has equipped others for the roles He's given them. Often, He'll have you work together, combining your gifts to produce a greater result.

Sometimes, working alongside people who are different from you can send you sliding into comparison or inadequacy. Remember, God put careful thought into which role He gave to each person and has created each one to fill their role well. Rather than viewing those who are different to you as a threat, try to see them through God's eyes. He has an equally important part for them to play in His body—and even in your life.

When you take on Jesus' yoke, you give Him permission to place you exactly where He wants you in His body. He'll help you grow into your role, setting the pace and teaching you to receive from others—even those you find difficult. Iron sharpening iron, Solomon calls it. Those times of rubbing up against others are often awkward and sometimes painful but if you want to be a sharp, effective instrument in God's hands, you need to be prepared for honing.

Beautiful woman of God, you are not expected to have all the answers or be everything to everyone. You are one member of a large body. All Jesus asks is that you embrace your place and learn to receive God's care and input through others. When you do, you'll discover the security and rest that come from knowing you're part of something much bigger than yourself.

Ask God to show you any mindsets that hinder you from experiencing rest in His body.

DAY 30:

Rest in His Boundaries

*'The righteous will flourish like a palm tree,
they will grow like a cedar of Lebanon;
planted in the house of the LORD,
they will flourish in the courts of our God.'*
Psalm 92:12-13

Have you ever felt restricted by God, like the limits He was placing on your life were too tight, too strict? Or did you go through a time when He extended your boundaries into territory you were reluctant to enter?

In Psalm 92, the writer says we flourish like beautiful, enduring, fruitful trees when we're planted within God's courts. The court mentioned in the above verses is not a royal court, with tiled floor, ornate throne and arching ceiling, but a court*yard*—an outdoor area surrounded by walls. The walls served to limit movement, protect insiders from enemies and extremes of weather, and set boundaries for the growth of the plants within.

God has a purpose for the boundaries of your life. Whether you're feeling restricted or stretched out of your comfort zone, His walls are there to protect, to guide you and to keep you from harm. In order to flourish within His boundaries you need to stay inside them, to accept where He's planted you. Sink your roots deep into His soil and draw on His rich nourishment. Then, out of that place of rest and strength in Him you'll blossom into the woman He created you to be.

Earlier in our journey I mentioned how God had taught me that yieldedness was the place of rest. Last year He added another layer to that picture. 'Yieldedness is the place of power.' Of course! It's only when we choose to follow God's guidance to do what may seem crazy or impossible that we have the opportunity to see His power manifest in our lives. It's only in our weakness that His power is made perfect (2 Corinthians 12:9).

Rest and power go hand in hand. When you rest in the boundaries God has set for you, you'll be empowered to flourish into all He created you to be. That blessing will flow on to your family and beyond, drawing others to know God through the beauty and fruitfulness they see in your life.

Where do you need to yield to God's boundaries so you can flourish?

Some Final Thoughts

Beautiful Mother,

Thanks for joining me on this 30-day journey. I hope you've gleaned a new understanding of God's desire to lead you into His rest. He wants your life to be infused with His peace and strength—for your wellbeing and the benefit of those around you.

When you live from a place of rest in God, your life becomes a resting place for others. Your family and friends, your colleagues and neighbours will all be blessed by the living water that flows from you as you continuously draw from God's deep well (John 7:38).

If this journey has been hard for you and you feel like you're still stuck in patterns of stress and striving, please don't give up. Breaking free of old ways of thinking and behaviour takes time. I've been on this journey for more than 12 years and I'm still learning! Keep choosing to draw near to God, meditate on the truth to renew your mind, and keep seeking to walk with Jesus. His rest will surely come. Though it may take a while for you to taste it, when it comes, you'll be glad you persevered.

The discussion on forgiveness in week two may have stirred some difficult memories. If you feel unsure how to work through them, you may find it helpful to read 'Steps in Forgiveness' in the next few pages. If the idea of walking with Jesus appeals to you but you haven't yet given your life to Him, please read 'How to Know Jesus'.

This devotional was birthed out of an online challenge I led for mothers in July 2022. Every minute with these precious ladies was a joy. Through Zoom and Facebook, we spent a full month delving into the many dimensions of God's rest. When the journey ended, I wanted to provide something tangible to help them continue on their journey. And so, this book was created.

The writing process has taken much longer than I expected and I've felt my level of rest being tested multiple times. Every time I stilled my heart and returned my gaze to God, He restored my peace and showed me the way forward. In every season, He is my anchor.

If you're interested in joining an online journey, I'd love to have you! I count it a privilege to dwell on and share these truths with other women. You can find out more at my website, thethrivinglife.org, under 'A 30 Day Journey into God's Rest for Mothers'.

As you close the pages of this book, my prayer is that this won't mark the end of a short season learning about rest but the beginning of a lifelong pursuit of intimacy with God. Always, there is more of Him to discover and enjoy.

> *'Taste and see that the LORD is good;*
> *Blessed is the one who takes refuge in Him.'*
>
> Psalm 34:8

With love,

Sue

*'My Presence will go with you,
and I will give you rest.'*

Exodus 33: 14

Steps in Forgiveness

In week two of this journey we discussed forgiveness—God's gracious forgiveness of you and your need to forgive others. While you may open your arms wide to receive God's great mercy, the idea of forgiving people who have wounded you may seem unfathomable.

Forgiveness began with God. He saw you drowning in your sin—separated from Him—and sent His Son, Jesus, to rescue you. Jesus offered Himself as a sacrifice in your place, taking the punishment for all your wrongdoing, and opened the way for you to be washed clean and warmly welcomed into God's family.

Nothing you did or could ever do would make you worthy of such grace. If you reflect on that truth, it can make forgiving others a little easier.

There are two steps in the process of forgiveness. Both are vital. First, acknowledge before God your own frailty and the ways you have caused pain for others. You may also need to take responsibility for any sinful reactions to the harm done to you, like bitterness or malice. As you confess, God will forgive and cleanse you from all your sin (1 John 1:9).

Next, acknowledge the pain and trauma others have caused you and make a choice to forgive them. This isn't something you do based on your feelings. It's an act of your will.

Take note: to forgive doesn't mean you are minimising the wrong done to you, nor does it mean you're opening the door to be hurt by that person again. It may be important to limit contact with them, bring the relationship to an end or even report them to authorities. All of this can be done with an attitude of forgiveness.

Once you forgive, you will be more able to let go of all the negative emotions which have gripped you since the incident. Once those emotions are dealt with, you'll be free to move forward in your life, enjoying a new level of lightness and intimacy with God.

If you find it difficult to go through this process alone, it may be helpful for you to enlist the support of a close friend, pastor or counsellor. I encourage you to be proactive in seeking freedom. Beyond the pain of this moment, God has a life of liberty waiting for you.

How to Know Jesus

I've been a church-going girl my entire life. From the age of three I went to Sunday School, then progressed to church once I reached my teens. I genuinely loved Jesus and longed to know Him personally. But I didn't know how. It wasn't until I was 16 that the process was explained to me.

It all begins with surrender.

God, our Creator, wants more than anything else for us to be close to Him but often we ignore Him and go our own way, thinking we know better. Sometimes we hide from Him, cowering under the pain and shame of our mistakes. Either way, this sin—this fear and rebellion—separates us from God.

God saw the mess we were in and knew we couldn't save ourselves. So, He sent His precious Son, Jesus, from heaven to earth to live among sinful people and show them what God was like. Jesus loved, healed and provided food for thousands and spoke words of truth that brought life and understanding. Many people put their hope in Him. Some turned their backs.

Jesus' life on earth ended abruptly when He was executed on a cross. It looked like His opponents had managed to crush Him. But God was working it all for good. Through His death, Jesus offered Himself as a sacrifice for all people, taking on the guilt and punishment for our sin and opening the way for us to know God. Three days later He rose again, showing His defeat of sin and death and Satan.

Now, He's giving you an invitation.

'Come,' He says. ***'Come to me with all your sin and fear and shame. I'll forgive you and wash you as white as snow. Surrender your life to me and I will make you new. Then, walk with Me and I'll teach you a new way of living.'*** (Isaiah 1:18, 2 Corinthians 5:17, Matthew 11:28-29)

You may have tried religion—a pattern of living that tells you what you must do to be acceptable to God. None of that is necessary. All you need to do is put your faith in Jesus and His sacrifice. You might pray something like this:

'Jesus, I believe in you. I believe you are the Son of God and you died to take the punishment for my sin. Thank you for dying for me. Lord, I'm sorry for all the ways I've sinned and tried to live without you. I don't want to live like that anymore. I surrender my life to you now. Thank you for forgiving me and washing me clean. Please fill me with your

Holy Spirit and teach me how to live this new life with you.'

If you prayed this prayer, congratulations! You have begun a new life as God's child and heaven is celebrating (Luke 15:7). Now you are free to run into Jesus' presence any time, to walk and talk with Him and to know His guidance and provision. Open your heart to Him each day and He'll walk with you, unfolding His plans for your life and leading you step by step.

I encourage you to find a Christian friend or contact a Christian church and tell them you've given your life to Jesus, so they can help you get a Bible and support you as you grow. And please message me on Facebook at Susan Brown Author or Instagram @ susanbrownauthor21, so I can celebrate with you.

*'My soul finds rest in God alone;
my salvation comes from him.
He alone is my rock and my salvation;
he is my fortress, I will never be shaken.'*

Psalm 62: 1

www.ingramcontent.com/pod-product-compliance
Lightning Source LLC
Chambersburg PA
CBHW020328010526
44107CB00054B/2029